THE FANTASTIC FLATULENT FART BROTHERS'

SECOND

BIG BOOK OF

FARTY FACTS

AN ILLUSTRATED GUIDE TO THE SCIENCE, HISTORY, ART, AND LITERATURE OF FARTING

by M.D. Whalen

illustrated by Florentino Gopez

First US edition, published 2018

Top Floor Books
imprint of stvdio media
PO Box 29
Silvermine Bay, Hong Kong

visit us at www.topfloorbooks.com

ISBN 978 962 7866 40 4

CONTENTS

INTRODUCTION

THEY DON'T TEACH you about farting in school. Which is kind of surprising.

After all, you're forced to study things like ancient Egypt and the periodic table. But when's the last time you pooted a pyramid? Has anyone ever stunk up a room with helium or argon gas?

Yet the body function that we perform every day, more often than eating or drinking, doesn't have a curriculum of its own.

How unfair!

Fart literature has been around since the ancient Greeks. The greatest American president told fart jokes. Royalty, religions, and music have been influenced by farts. There's a real movie award for Best Fart.

Fossils fart. Inhaling farts was a cure for the Great Plague. Moths kill by farting, yet kangaroo farts could save the planet.

So put aside that school book. Turn off that science show. Peel open these pages and raise your Fart IQ, in the fascinating and funny world of intestinal gas.

SECTION ONE

FARTS IN THE NEWS

4

Kids Jailed for Farting

IN THE AMERICAN town of Meridian, Mississippi, kids went to prison for farting in class!

The Meridian school district wanted to finally put a stop to student misbehavior. Such crimes included wearing the wrong color socks to class, using bad language, or worst of all, the felony of flatulence.

Instead of sending guilty farters to the principal, teachers were told to call the police. Students were hauled away in handcuffs just for ripping a stinker in class.

The American Civil Liberties Union and the US Department of Justice finally sued the school district over such cruel and unusual punishment. The school district lost.

Thanks to this case, farting is now protected by law. Next time someone complains about your gas, explain that you are merely exercising your Constitutional right to fart.

Fart Tax Protest

IN SEPTEMBER 2003, New Zealand farmers raised a stink at plans to impose the world's first "fart tax" on livestock emissions.

Nicknamed the "back-door tax", the money was intended to fund research into reducing the 37 million tons of methane spewed into the atmosphere each year by New Zealand's livestock. With thirty million sheep and ten million cows all farting buckets, it's a wonder anyone there can breathe.

Hundreds of farmers used tractors to block the streets of the nation's capital, Wellington, in protest. Cows were led up the steps of the Parliament building, where their own feelings could be heard, and smelled.

The tax proposal didn't pass, allowing gas to pass instead, tax-free, from New Zealand's cows and sheep.

Barn Burner

WHEN AN ENTIRE building explodes without warning, don't blame terrorists. Blame cow farts.

That's what happened in Rasdorf, Germany, in January 2014, when ninety cows stuck inside a barn blew the place apart.

Cows release highly flammable methane from both ends, and they release a lot! When you put so many cows together, farting in a closed space, just one little spark will turn it into a bomb.

If you've ever scuffed your feet across a carpet on a dry day, you may have felt a shock of static electricity. In this case, a couple of cows rubbed each other the wrong way. According to the Rasdorf Police, "a static electric charge caused the gas to explode with flashes of flames."

Luckily, only one cow suffered minor injuries, though the barn was destroyed. And the farmer may have discovered a new way to make whipped cream.

Crazy Toot Trial

IS FARTING A form of assault? The police in Berlin, Germany, think so.

In February 2016, Berlin Police approached a group of young people and demanded to see their identity cards. In protest, one man aimed a fart at the police. When he farted a second time, the officer became furious.

A full year later, the accused farter was fined €900 (around US$1065) for the crime of assaulting a police officer. He refused to pay and was hauled into court.

The trial raised a big stink, even in the government, where a Berlin Senator criticized the police for wasting countless man-hours just to prosecute a man for farting.

The news media labeled it the *Irrer-Pups Prozess* (the "Crazy Toot Trial"). Despite the ridiculousness of it all, the trial went ahead. One wonders how the police intended to present the evidence.

The judge didn't want to find out. He dismissed the case after just ten minutes.

Swedish Squealers

IN 2010, A Swedish convict protested against harsh prison conditions by farting at the guards. The prison's warden claimed that such repeated episodes of flatulence were "a series of attacks" on staff.

Defending his actions, the 21-year-old inmate said, "I had an upset stomach while I was playing cards but did not want to fart there. So I went over to the guards instead."

He received a warning over his putrid protest. And presumably, beans were removed from the prison menu.

COULD HE BE the same Swedish guy who, six years later, was charged with criminal farting by his ex-girlfriend?

According to her official complaint, the man was visiting her apartment. When the woman ordered him to get out, he left behind a foul-smelling fart in revenge.

The local police declined to follow the case. "It's impossible to prove that he wanted to pass particularly smelly wind on purpose," they said.

Perhaps they were worried about fart protests in the interrogation room.

The Fart Before Christmas

You better watch out
You better not cry
You better not pout
I'm telling you why
Santa Claus is farting downtown

AND THEN GETTING beaten up for it.

In December 2012, a guy was coming out of a bar in Omaha, Nebraska. Just outside, a man dressed as Saint Nick decided it is better to give than to receive: he lifted a leg and gave the passerby a huge honking fart.

Santa received something in return: a big fat punch in the face.

"I was just trying to enjoy myself as Santa Claus. You know, spread good cheer," Santa said. "I mean, can you not free range fart in public?"

The guy who punched him said he was proud to beat up Santa Claus if it would help people enjoy the festive season without Saint Nick's bottom-bursting ho-ho-ho's.

We can guess who Santa moved from the Nice list to the Naughty list that year.

FARTY ANIMALS

Fossil Farts

BIOLOGISTS AT THE University of Massachusetts recently discovered the oldest farts on earth: 20 million years old, in fact. And they still stink.

While studying prehistoric termites trapped in amber, they noticed tiny bubbles around the fossilized insects. The scientists drilled into the bubbles and analyzed the gases. These turned out to be mainly methane and carbon dioxide, the main ingredients of intestinal gas.

They also found fossilized gut bacteria inside the termites' intestines. Which proves they were farting.

It's well-known that termites are the gassiest creatures on earth. The scientists therefore concluded that these ancient insects had been feasting on a tree, got stuck in its sap, and let out cheesers from their last meal while the resin hardened around them.

It eventually turned into amber, preserving their poots for all time.

Fart Bird

PARTRIDGES DON'T LIVE in pear trees (they are ground dwellers). But they are named after farts.

The word partridge is based on the ancient Greek word, *perdesthai,* which means "to fart". It seems that some ancient Greek bird watcher heard a bird flapping its wings in the bushes, thought it sounded like a fart, and named it the Fart Bird.

Then shouldn't it be called *fart*-ridge instead?

Dog Fart Science

RESEARCHERS AT THE Waltham Center for Pet Nutrition in England are so interested in dog farts, they simply had to study them.

They dressed dogs in a specially-designed suit, with a little hole in the rear, where they captured dog butt emissions for analysis.

Then some lucky research assistant was appointed as Odor Judge. Their job was to smell and rate each dog fart on a stink scale of 1 to 5.

What did they find? Dog fart smell, just like in humans, is mainly caused by hydrogen sulfide.

These intrepid scientists couldn't get enough of dog farts, so they did a follow-up study!

They experimented with making dog farts less stinky. Dogs were fed different substances. Then the poor Odor Judge once again stuck his nose behind the pooting pooches.

The scientists concluded that adding charcoal and zinc to their food reduces dog fart stink.

Please don't try this at home! One researcher warned that feeding your dog too much charcoal or zinc might harm its health.

You're free, however, to be a Dog Fart Odor Judge at home.

Pennsylvania Cat Farts

CATS FART MUCH less than dogs. And most of the time you can't hear them.

Cat digestive systems are very efficient when processing meat. If your cat farts, it's probably caused by fillers in dry cat food, like soybeans or corn. And you may want to hold back on giving kitty that saucer of milk, since cow's milk can raise quite a storm in his or her belly. But the number one cause of cat farts is air swallowed when a cat gobbles its food too fast.

If your kitty cat raises a death-defying stink, it's no laughing matter. It could be a sign of gut disease, so you might want to ask your vet to give it a whiff.

CATS APPARENTLY FART more in Pennsylvania. According to researchers, the Google search term "Do cats fart?" is asked more often by people in Pennsylvania than in any other US state.

The researchers didn't explain *why* anyone needed to know where cats fart the most.

Pig Fart Emergency

LATE ONE NIGHT in November 2009, fire trucks rushed to a farm in Axedale, Australia, after reports of a potentially dangerous gas leak. But the gas they discovered wasn't coming from metal or plastic pipes.

The Fire Captain said: "As we drove up the driveway, there was this huge sow, about a 120-odd kilo (265-pound) sow, and it was very obvious where the gas was coming from. We could not only smell it, but we heard it, and it was quite funny. She squealed and farted and squealed and farted."

The Fire Captain and his fifteen volunteer firefighters laughed: "I haven't heard too many pigs fart, but I would describe it as very full-on."

Turtle Fart Alarm

TURTLE FARTS NEARLY spoiled Christmas at a British aquarium park.

A resident turtle at Weymouth Sea Life Adventure Park in England was rewarded with a holiday treat of Brussels sprouts. Then he went for a swim.

The happy terrapin soon passed wind near the edge of the aquarium tank. Its fart bubbles rose to the surface, where they popped and splashed onto a water level sensor. This set off a false alarm that the 132,000 gallon (500,000 liter) tank was overflowing.

Aquarium workers rushed to the scene. The tooting turtle must have still been spewing up a storm, because they quickly got to the bottom of the matter.

"Sprouts are a healthy Christmas treat for sea turtles," a marine biologist at the park explained. "But they give similar side effects to those experienced by humans."

Green Kangaroo Farts

KANGAROOS HAVE 'GREEN' farts. But that has nothing to do with the color.

Kangaroo farts are more environmentally friendly than other animals' gut gas. They contain the lowest amounts of methane, a gas that contributes to global warming.

Cow and sheep farts are often blamed for a large portion of the methane in the earth's atmosphere. Therefore, scientists thought that kangaroo flatulence was worth studying. Perhaps the bacteria in kangaroo guts could be transplanted into cows and solve the climate change problem.

Researchers from Australia and Switzerland kept two different species of kangaroos in comfortable sealed chambers, where they analyzed the food going in and gases coming out.

It turns out that stomach microbes have little to do with the content of their farts. Kangaroos just digest their food more efficiently. They don't fart less, they simply fart differently.

The researchers did not report what green farts smell like.

Death by Moth Fart

A MOTH KNOWN as the Beaded Lacewing has the deadliest butt gas on the planet.

These moths lay their eggs in termite nests.

As the baby moths get bigger, and hungrier, they release farts which knock dead any nearby termites, which then become snacks for the greedy baby moths.

For reasons that scientists can't explain, Beaded Lacewing farts are deadly only to termites, and not to other small creatures often hanging around nearby, such as spiders and centipedes.

But to be on the safe side, hold your breath next time a moth flutters past.

Mermaid Farts

WHEN CHRISTOPHER COLUMBUS arrived in the Americas, he discovered manatees.

Columbus mistook these gentle aquatic animals for mermaids. Maybe he wouldn't have found them so enchanting if he knew that manatees fart all day long.

Manatees, who live in shallow, marshy water, eat between 100 and 150 pounds (45 to 68 kg) of vegetation each day. Which means a lot of methane builds up in their guts. Instead of letting it out for pleasure, they store the gas inside huge bladders in their bodies.

If they want to dive deeper, they let rip a big bubbly blast, which makes them heavier in the water. When they want to float back to the top they simply hold it in.

Next time you're caught farting in a public swimming pool, simply explain that you're imitating manatees, for science.

National Chicken Farts

IN CHINA, CHICKEN farts are a form of protest. Not real chicken farts, but the word itself.

The Chinese government likes to boast about its Gross Domestic Product, or GDP, which is a term used to measure the country's economy. Many Chinese people think that their government is more concerned about the country's GDP than about the environment or worker safety.

When spoken out loud, the abbreviation "GDP" sounds like the Chinese word *jee de pee* 鸡的屁, which means "chicken farts".

This has inspired some clever protests. People post messages on Weibo–the Chinese version of Twitter–saying things like:

What's more important, clean water or chicken farts?

We want blue skies, not chicken farts!

Sadly, Chinese officials plug their ears, and their noses, at such comments.

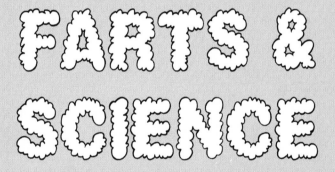

Farting Plants

EVEN PLANTS FART, and are quite rude about it.

Mimosa pudica is called the Sensitive Plant, because of the way its leaves fold up when touched. But they might as well rename it the *In*sensitive Plant.

This plant will fart if you feel its roots. Tiny sacs at its bottom end release a foul-smelling gas when touched. It's probably a defense reaction to repel animals seeking a salad lunch.

The Sensitive Plant isn't alone. *Jacobaea vulgaris,* which grows in northern Europe, is called *vulgar* for a reason. If you rub its leaves, they (and your fingers) stink like a horse's butt. No wonder its common name is the Mare's Fart, and in some places it's called the Stinking Willie.

Then there's the Cotton Thistle, a purple wild flower. Its scientific name, *Onopordum acanthium,* comes from the Greek words *ónos* (donkey) and *pérdo* (to fart). Yes indeed: it's the Donkey Fart flower. This isn't because of its smell, but its noticeable effect on donkeys who graze on it.

Three plants to leave out of your Mother's Day bouquet!

Shower Stink

DID YOU EVER notice that your farts smell worse in the shower? Go try it right now...

Done? Did they smell especially rotten? Here's why.

Most of the time, we don't mind the smell of our own farts. Since the chemical makeup of our excretions comes from our own bodies, we tend to not notice the smell very much. Same for when we sweat.

That all changes when we're cleaning ourselves. A shower or bath magnifies and even changes the stench of our farts.

Scientists of course have several explanations.

One is that the stink molecules bind to the water vapor, which alters their chemistry and so you notice the smell. The other reason is that the vapor fills your nostrils and filters out odors. Therefore, in response, the olfactory nerves inside your nose turn up their sensitivity.

Either way, always avoid taking a shower right after somebody who's just eaten a bean and onion burrito.

Fart Sniffing Robot

CHINESE SCIENTISTS INVENTED a robot which answers the age-old question: "Who farted?"

It's called the Odor Source Localization Machine. The robot uses smell detectors, combined with information about a room's air flow, to trace the source of any aroma.

It was originally designed to locate dangerous gas leaks in factories. But Chinese state news knows better. Their headline reported that the machine "solves the mystery of who farted."

The fart sniffing robot was considered so ground-breaking (or wind-breaking?) that the OSLM received one of China's top science prizes.

The perfect robot for your next family gathering.

Sweet Farts

WHY DO FARTS have a bad name? They feel great. They make people laugh. They're natural. Oh yeah...

They stink.

An inventor in France has come up with the solution. Based on ten years of research, Christian Poincheval developed pills which make your farts smell nice. Choose from roses, violets, chocolate, or ginger. He even has fart powder for dogs.

Trouble is: from now on, every time you smell roses, does this mean someone farted?

And think of the effect it will have on poetry:

Roses are farts
Violets are poo
I fart in your face
To prove I love you

HOWARD PREPARES
CHRISTMAS
PRESENTS

Fart Collecting

WANT TO JOIN the exciting new hobby of fart collecting? The best way is to do it in the bathtub.

Fill a jar with bath water and then hold it with the open end downward. Lean back in the tub so that your fart bubbles come out in front, where you can see them. Catch the bubbles in the jar, and put on the lid while it's still upside down underwater. This way, you capture a pure fart uncontaminated by air.

To be a truly professional fart collector, choose the proper container. Believe it or not, there has been research about this!

Hydrogen sulfide and other odor-causing fart gases react with glass, rubber, and some plastics, and therefore lose their potency. But you're in luck: farts will retain their aroma in polypropylene food containers, available in many supermarkets.

Save your farts for posterity. Let your great-grandchildren know how much you stink!

FART MEDICINE

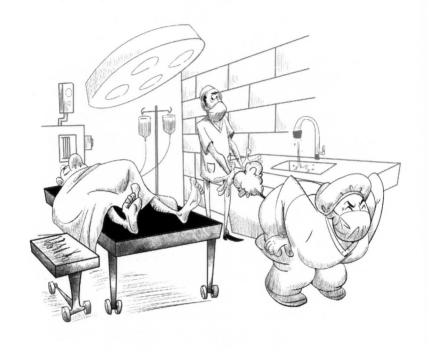

SURGERY ROOM HAND SANITIZER

Nurse Farts

AN AUSTRALIAN NURSE worried that her farts in the operating room might cause infections in her patients. When she mentioned this to the doctor, he decided to find out.

He had people fart into petri dishes, both with and without their pants pulled down.

The dishes from the naked farts grew bacteria. But these were the kinds of germs found on most people's skin, and which are no more harmful than the bacteria used to make yogurt.

The farts from people with pants on came out clean.

In other words, the germs were not from the farts themselves, but were blown from the skin around people's butts. With clothes on, these microbes were filtered out by the fabric.

The doctor reported: "Our final conclusion? Don't fart naked near food. All right, it's not rocket science. But then again, maybe it is?"

Fart Jars

THE GREAT PLAGUE of London from 1665 to 1666 killed 100,000 people, a quarter of the city's population. They could have been saved by their own farts!

At the time, people didn't realize that the plague was a disease spread by flea bites. Experts believed that the plague was a deadly invisible vapor in the air that you caught by inhaling it. Doctors claimed that you could dilute the infected air by breathing in something even more foul, the stinkier the better. In other words, they prescribed farts.

Some people kept goats inside their homes and let them stink up the place. But many people farted into jars and kept them handy, so they could quickly fill their lungs with butt gas any time they thought they might have been exposed to the plague.

There are no reports of how many people's lives were saved by breathing in bottled farts. But three-quarters of London's inhabitants managed to survive, so make your own conclusion.

Start saving your farts in jars, for the next time you feel some sniffles coming on.

Toot Tracker

FINALLY, THERE'S AN electronic device that lets you track your farts from the inside, on your very own phone.

Australian medical researchers developed a tiny pill-shaped sensing device that measures the gas in your guts.

First you swallow it. As the sensor travels through your stomach and intestines, it takes readings about the levels of various gases, then wirelessly sends this information to a nearby computer or mobile device. Then you can track your fart's size and movements on an app.

What's the point? They say doctors can use it to pinpoint the location of any unusual activity in your digestive system. On the other hand, maybe they just want to be warned when a patient is about to cut a cheeser inside the examination room.

Either way, this is the year's must-have gadget!

FARTS

IN

HISTORY

Sir Henry the Farter

A HEATED DEBATE in the English Parliament in 1607 turned rancid, when Sir Henry Ludlow farted so loudly that it echoed throughout the chambers.

Sir Henry's fart became he stuff of legends. It inspired a poem called "The Censure of the Parliament Fart".

Here's an excerpt (using modern spelling):

Never was bestowed such art
Upon the tuning of a Fart.
Well, quoth Sir Henry Poole, it was a bold trick
To Fart in the nose of the body politic
Thank God, quoth Sir Edward Hungerford,
That this Fart proved not a Turd
Quoth Sir Jerome in folio, I swear by the Mass
This Fart was enough to have broken all my Glass
Such a Fart was never seen
Quoth the Learned Council of the Queen.
A good year on this fart, quoth gentle Sir Harry,
He has caused such an Earthquake that my coal
    pits miscarry.

The Forgotten Fart

EDWARD DE VERE, the 17th Earl of Oxford, was well-known as a poet, playwright, and supporter of the arts.

He was also a supporter of the farts.

In the late 1500s he was a welcome guest in the palace of Queen Elizabeth the First. But in 1581 he was banished from the court. A historian of the time explains:

This Earl, bowing to Queen Elizabeth, happened to let a fart, at which he was so abashed and ashamed that he went to travel for seven years.

Back in London, deeply in debt, and crippled from too many sword fights, the repentant Earl was at last allowed to visit the royal court again. According to the historian, the Queen had forgiven him:

On his return the Queen welcomed him home and said, "My Lord, I had forgotten the fart."

Abe Lincoln's Fart Jokes

ABRAHAM LINCOLN MAY have freed the slaves and saved the Union. But what made him truly the greatest US President? Easy: he told fart jokes!

Here's one of Lincoln's actual gassy gags:

Well there was a party once, not far from here, composed of ladies and gentlemen. A fine table was set and the people were greatly enjoying themselves.

Among the crowd was one of those men who had audacity. After the men and women had enjoyed themselves by dancing, promenading, flirting, etc., they were told that the table was set. The man of audacity was put at the head of the table to carve the turkeys, chickens, and pigs.

The men and women surrounded the table, and the audacious man commenced carving the turkey, but he expended too much force and let a fart—a loud fart so that all the people heard it distinctly.

A deep silence reigned. The man pulled off his coat, rolled up his sleeves, spat on his hands, and picked up the carving knife, never moving a muscle of his face. It became a wonder in the minds of all the men and women how the fellow was to get out of his dilemma.

He squared himself and said loudly and distinctly: "Now, by God, I'll see if I can't cut up this turkey without farting."

Fart at the French

IN 2014 BRITAIN declared war on France with a fart across the English Channel. Or at least one British man did.

Inventor Colin Furze (whose last name, incidentally, means "fart" in German) decided to take a shot at England's ancient enemy across the Channel. He created a gigantic mechanical farting butt, which he placed on the cliffs of Dover, and aimed it directly at France.

On July 25, 2014, Furze's fartillery blasted a massive bowel burner!

Did it work?

The inventor claims that two French people on the other side of the water reported hearing the titanic toot, though they didn't smell a thing.

Every war inspires patriotic songs, and this stinker of a battle is no exception. A song called "Fart at the French" was recorded and, appropriately, plopped off the bottom of the pop charts.

SECTION SIX

FAMOUS FARTERS

Queen of Farts

WHEN QUEEN VICTORIA was in charge, the sun never set on the British Empire. Apparently, it also never set on her farting.

The Queen liked to wolf down six-course meals without pausing for breath. It's no wonder that she constantly complained of indigestion.

It was also no surprise when an Australian journalist wrote that the Queen was "fat, flabby, and flatulent." She sued him for libel and lost. Maybe the judge was able to smell the evidence.

One evening after another sumptuous meal, the Queen was convinced she was having a heart attack. Her personal physician rushed in and examined her. He reassured the frightened dinner guests that it was only gas pains:

"I fancy Her Majesty had flatulence."

As if they couldn't smell it for themselves.

Mozart: A Little Fart Music

YOU THINK CLASSICAL music is boring? You wouldn't say that about Wolfgang Amadeus Mozart.

The greatest of all composers wrote a song for a six-voice choir called "Leck mich am Arsch" ("Lick my butt"). He composed at least two other songs with similar lyrics.

Mozart was well-known for having a potty mouth, which often got him in trouble. In a letter to his cousin, he described hearing a noise and smelling a foul stench which he couldn't find the source of, until he stuck his finger in his own butt and held it to his nose.

Mozart loved poop and fart jokes so much, he even wrote this masterpiece of a poem in a letter to his own mother:

Yesterday, though, we heard the king of farts
It smelled as sweet as honey tarts
While it wasn't in the strongest of voice
It still came on as a powerful noise.

Now, that's some classical gas!

Pooting Stars

CELEBRITIES FART JUST like normal people. But a few stars really puff out from the crowd.

BRITNEY SPEARS

The pop singer was sued by her bodyguard, for constantly picking her nose and farting in front of him. He described her farts as a "lethal weapon." The superstar's lawyer claimed that she couldn't help producing such toxic gas because she suffered from a rare disease called Flatulencia Explotatta (which doesn't exist).

Spears at least admits that she farts. On British television, asked whether she ever farted on stage, she held up a sign saying, "Oops...I did it."

WHOOPI GOLDBERG

A comedian named Caryn Johnson farted so often that her friends said she was a living whoopee cushion. So she started calling herself Whoopi. And she's never stopped with the gas. During a 2014 TV appearance, she let out a massive fart that sent other people scrambling.

MARILYN MONROE

The top 1950s movie actress apparently farted so much that Clark Gable, her co-star in her last film, didn't want to come anywhere near her.

FARTS &
ENTERTAINMENT

Royal Farter

IMAGINE FARTING FOR a living—in front of the king!

That was the job of one lucky fellow, known as Roland le Fartere, or Roland the Farter.

Back in twelfth century England, whenever King Henry II needed some cheering up, he summoned his court jester, Roland the Farter, to release the tension, and the gas.

Every year, Roland put on a Christmas show for the entire royal court, in which the king required him to jump around and whistle, and perform what was politely called a "bumbulum".

In return Roland was given a manor house and 30 acres (12 hectares) of land.

He must have held it in all year to produce such a well-paid fart.

French Fartiste

JOSEPH PUJOL WAS the most famous farter ever.

Born in France in 1857, as a child he realized he could suck in water through his rear end and squirt it back out. With practice, he learned to pull in air to play tunes through his butt. He was popular in school, and later in the army, where his fellow soldiers gave him the nickname *Le Pétomane,* which translates as The Fartist.

He tried a "normal" career as a baker. But at age 30 he stepped on stage in Marseilles wearing a fine red suit, bent over, and revealed his talents as *fartiste extraordinaire.* Soon he was a headline act at Paris's famous Moulin Rouge theater.

His act of *petomanie*—or "fartistry"—consisted of fart impressions of famous people, tooting out songs, blowing out candles, even imitating cannons and thunderstorms. After an intermission, he smoked cigarettes and played musical instruments through a tube in his butt.

Audiences went wild. Le Pétomane became a superstar, the highest-paid entertainer in all of France. Surprisingly, his farts didn't stink, since he cleaned out his colon before every show.

When he died at 88, a medical school requested to examine the world's most famous anus, but his family refused, stating: "some things in this life simply must be treated with reverence."

Irish Rectal Music

IRELAND'S ANCIENT GAELIC chieftains enjoyed a bit of fun at their feasts, including musicians, jugglers, jesters, and performers who pulled down their pants for comical effect.

But the star of the show was the *braigetoir,* or professional farter.

Luckily we have pictorial proof. In 1578, an Englishman named John Derricke wrote an illustrated account of one such party. One drawing shows a chieftain and his men enjoying dinner and drinks while two professional farters bare their butts at the host.

There's an idea for your next St. Patrick's Day bash!

84

Fart Songs

ARE YOU SICK and tired of most pop songs being about love-love-love? Sing fart songs instead!

That's what English people did back in the 1650s. The church banned popular songs. Only religious songs were allowed in public.

This made many musicians angry. So they set up private clubs where, in protest, they sang the rudest songs they could come up with.

One popular hit was "My Lady and Her Maid":

My lady and her Maid
Upon a merry pin,
They made a match at farting
Who should the wager win.

Joan lights three candles then
And sets them bolt upright,
With the first fart she blew them out,
With the next she gave them light.

One composer, Thomas D'Urfey, wrote numerous songs about farting women, including his #1 chart-topper, "The Fart, Famous for its Satyrical Humour in the Reign of Queen Anne".

Jonathan Swift, author of *Gulliver's Travels* (and an essay about farts), described D'Urfey's music as "excrement". Was that meant to be praise or criticism?

Fart Symphony

AN AUSTRALIAN MUSICIAN discovered just how musical flatulence can be. One of his toots turned out to be a symphony in disguise.

In 2015 he recorded his own fart, then slowed down the playback. He found that a single butt blast was composed of seven distinct notes. In musical terms, they formed a major seventh arpeggio in B flat with an incidental at the end.

The rest is musical history. He turned his fart into a symphony for full orchestra, which he called his Rectum Opus. It's had millions of views on YouTube.

The composer fears that his best work is behind him.

Farts on the Silver Screen

BEST MOVIE FART: yes, this was a real award!

Nickelodeon's Kids Choice Awards in 2003 and 2004 included the category "Best Fart in a Movie", as well as an award for "Best Burp".

The 2003 winner was the "Scooby Doo" movie; 2004's was "Kangaroo Jack".

Farts have a long and proud tradition in movies. Here are some other famous film farts:

- RAIN MAN: The famous fart-inside-a-telephone-booth scene, with Tom Cruise's classic line: "Did you just fart, man?"

- DUMB & DUMBER: One fart scene after another, after another, including Jim Carrey lighting a fart on fire.

- BLAZING SADDLES: Guess what makes the saddles blaze? Almost non-stop farting, including the unforgettable farts-around-the-campfire scene.

- SUPERHERO MOVIE: The funniest granny fart in cinematic history.

- THE NUTTY PROFESSOR: A fart dinner scene so gross you'll puke in your popcorn.

FART LITERATURE

Greek Reek

ANCIENT GREEKS LOVED fart jokes in popular entertainment 2500 years before "South Park".

In Aristophanes's play "The Clouds", Socrates explains that thunder is actually heavenly farts:

> *If a little tummy like yours can let off a fart like that, what do you think an infinity of air can do? That's how thunder comes about. In fact, I happen to know that in Phrygian—the oldest language on earth—they actually call thunder "phartos."*

In the play "Platus", Cario steals food from a temple, until a woman there "let flee a fart in her fear, which stank worse than a weasel." Afterward, Cario explains to his wife:

> *Such a good joke happened. My belly was quite blown up, and I let a thunderous fart!*

And in "The Frogs", Dionysus tries to row a boat through a crowd of rude frogs. He threatens over and over: "You know, my butt's starting to hurt...in a second it's going to..." Each time, the frogs finish his sentence with fart-like croaks.

Dionysus finally farts in the face of his rowing mate, then tells a story about a runner who blew out the Olympic torch with a fart.

It's not what they teach you in literature class!

Arabian Night Farts

THE ARABIAN NIGHTS, or *Tales of 1001 Nights,* gave us Aladdin, Sindbad the Sailor, and flying carpets. But one story genuinely reeks.

THE TALE OF ABU HASSAN

Abu Hassan married the lovely daughter of Baghdad's highest official. After an elaborate wedding and feast, Abu Hassan prepared to join his bride in the palace bed chamber. But he'd eaten and drunk so much that as he sat up, he released a loud and thundering fart that echoed from wall to wall and silenced every voice in the room.

Abu Hassan was so ashamed that he sneaked out of the palace, leaped on a horse to the coast and boarded a ship for India. There he served as guard to a rajah. But ten years later, he badly missed home. He returned to Baghdad, hoping that after such a long time his foul deed had been forgotten.

Just before entering the city gates, he overheard a woman putting her child to sleep.

The child asked, "Mama, when was I born?"

"That's easy, my dear," Mama said. "It was the year that Abu Hassan farted."

Abu Hassan fled the land and was never seen again.

Divine Flatulence

DANTE'S *DIVINE COMEDY* is considered one of the greatest works of world literature. Well, no wonder—it has fart jokes!

In the first volume, *The Inferno,* Dante and his travel companion Virgil are on a tour of the Underworld, where they run into a band of devils. One demon wants to poke Dante in the tush with a pitchfork.

The devil commander doesn't like the idea. Instead, he aims his heinous anus at Dante and grunts out a gasser.

They wheeled round by the dike on the left;
but first each pressed his tongue
between his teeth at their leader for a signal
and he made a trumpet of his rump.

That must have stunk like...well, you get it.

Cheesy Chaucer

HERE'S SOMETHING THEY never teach in English class.

The first fart gags ever published in English appeared in *The Canterbury Tales,* written by Geoffrey Chaucer in the 14th century.

This one is from "The Miller's Tale", in which Nicholas farts at Absolom, who then takes revenge by branding Nick's buttocks with hot metal.*

> *This Nicholas just then let fly a fart*
> *As loud as it had been a thunder-clap,*
> *And almost blinded Absolom, old chap;*
> *But he was ready with his hot iron*
> *And Nicholas right in the ass he got.*
> *Off went the skin a hand's-width about*
> *The blade burned his bottom so, throughout*
> *That for the pain he thought he should die*
> *And like one mad he started to cry*
> *"Help! Water! Water! For God's dear heart!"*

* *transcribed in modern English*

Rumbling Rabelais

GARGANTUA AND PANTAGRUEL, written in the 16th century by French author François Rabelais, is widely considered to be the world's first fantasy novel. It's also one of the first *fart*-asy novels.

In one chapter, a giant releases a bowel blast so powerful that the ground shakes and little people fly out his behind:

With the fart he blew the earth trembled for twenty-seven miles round, and with the fetid air of it he engendered more than fifty-three thousand little men, misshapen dwarfs.

One wonders what those little men have written on their birth certificates.

THE BENEFITS OF FARTING
IN LILLIPUT

Lilli-poot

LONG BEFORE HE wrote *Gulliver's Travels,* the Irish author and satirist Jonathan Swift penned a more pungent piece: *The Benefit of Farting Explain'd.*

Instead of using his real name, he called himself Obadiah Fizle, Groom of the Stool to the Princess of Arse-Mini in Sardinia.

He claimed that the essay was originally written in Spanish by Don Fartinando Puff-Indorst, Professor of Bumbast in the University of Crackow, which he "translated into English at the Request and for the Use of the Lady Damp-Fart, of Her-fart-shire."

The essay explains that holding in farts is dangerous because they might rise up into your brain. "Distempers are due to flatulences not adequately vented."

In other words, everyone should fart more.

Such profound advice might have helped Gulliver in Lilli-poot.

Franklin Farts Proudly

WHEN BENJAMIN FRANKLIN wasn't busy co-authoring the Declaration of Independence and US Constitution or flying kites in thunderstorms, he was busy writing about farts.

In 1781 he published "Fart Proudly", an essay which begins:

It is universally well known, That in digesting our common Food, there is created or produced in the Bowels of human Creatures, a great Quantity of Wind. That the permitting this Air to escape and mix with the Atmosphere, is usually offensive to the Company, from the fetid Smell that accompanies it.

The essay argues that there is a need for scientific research into all aspects of farting, including how to make farts stink less.

Franklin's fascination with flatulence didn't stop there. He's also responsible for these immortal words of wisdom:

He that lives upon hope will die farting.

Ben Franklin may be best known as one of America's Founding Fathers, but he stands alone as America's Founding Farter.

Hemingway's Heart Fart

ERNEST HEMINGWAY IS considered one of the greatest American writers of all time. Obviously because he wrote fart poems, such as this literary masterpiece:

Home is where the heart is,
Home is where the fart is.
Come let us fart in the home.
There is no art in a fart.
Still a fart may not be artless.
Let us fart and artless fart in the home.

A Fart Parable

BEN SIRA WAS an ancient wise man so powerful he could even cure farts. This parable appears in a medieval Jewish text, *The Alphabet of Sira*:

One day the King complained to Ben Sira, "My daughter farts 1000 times an hour. What can I do?"

Ben Sira replied, "Send her to me in the morning, and I will cure her."

When the princess showed up the next day, Ben Sira acted very upset and told her, "Your father ordered that I must expel 1000 farts in his presence three days from now, or he'll put me to death."

"Don't worry," the princess said. "I'll go in your place and let out 1000 farts in front of him."

"Thank you," said Ben Sira. "But to make sure, stay here for three days without breaking wind, so your farts will be saved up and ready on the third day."

Every time she felt a fart coming, the king's daughter followed Ben Sira's advice: she stood on one foot and closed her back-end "mouth". For three days no farts came from her behind.

On the third day Ben Sira took her to the King, saying, "Go and expel 1000 farts."

The princess stood before her father, but she was unable to fart even once.

The King stood up and kissed Ben Sira.

The Zen of Farting

SU DONGPO WAS an ancient Chinese poet, and a devout Buddhist. One day he wrote a poem:

I bow my head to the heaven within heaven
Hairline rays illuminating the universe
The eight winds cannot move me
Sitting still upon the purple golden lotus

The *eight winds* were: praise, ridicule, honor, disgrace, gain, loss, pleasure, and misery. Su meant that he was so enlightened, that such "winds" no longer affected him.

He sent his poem to Zen Master Foyin, who lived across the river. Su expected the Zen Master to praise him for his spiritual purity.

The next day, the Master sent the poem back, with the word "fart" written on it.

Angry at this insult, Su Dongpo leaped into a ferry to the other shore to demand an apology.

He found a note pinned to the Master's door:

The eight winds cannot move me
One fart blows me across the river

The Master's meaning was clear. If Su was so pure, unaffected by the *eight winds*, then why was he so easily angered by one small word?

Embarrassed but wiser, the poet left quietly.
A single fart had truly enlightened him.

Farts vs. Devils

FARTS PLAYED A role in founding the Protestant Church.

Martin Luther was a monk who tried to reform the Catholic Church. He was kicked out by the Pope not only for his radical teachings, but also, it seems, for his love of fart gags.

Most priests advocate prayer for fighting the Devil. But Martin Luther wrote:

I resist the devil, and often it is with a fart that I chase him away.

His sermons included such saintly wisdom as:

A happy fart never comes from a miserable ass.

But the great Christian reformer was better known for his colorful insults. When the Pope objected to the revolutionary ideas coming out of Martin Luther's mouth, Luther responded:

Which mouth do you mean? The one from which the farts come? You can keep that yourself!

He concluded by calling the Holy Father of the Roman Catholic Church "Pope Fart-ass".

That was the final straw. Was the greatest split in religious history caused by a fart joke?

Northern Farts

THE INUIT PEOPLE of northeastern Canada worship intestinal gas.

Their most powerful religious spirit is Matshishkapeu, whose name literally means "Fart Man". He speaks to his people with holy toots.

During tribal gatherings, every fart is believed to contain a message from Matshishkapeu. When any man releases a rump ripper, everyone else immediately shuts up so they can concentrate on its profound and pungent message. A tribal elder then announces the fart's true meaning.

Beware of making Fart Man angry. He might do what he did to another god, the Caribou Master, and curse you with a powerful case of constipation.

You can guess how these northern people say grace, although they wait until after eating. The Inuit consider it good manners to fart after a meal, to show appreciation and gratitude to the cook and to one gassy god.

Glory to Farts

SOME RELIGIONS BREAK bread, while others break wind.

In Morocco, it's believed that farts are the devil's work. Pooting inside a mosque will blind or even kill the angels living there. Anywhere a fart occurs is covered with a small pile of stones, to trap those evil, smelly spirits inside.

In Turkey, there's a proverb about gut gas: "If the imam farts, the congregation will poop." Meaning: when a leader sets a bad example, the followers will do worse. Hopefully, Turkish clergy don't eat beans before a service.

What happens when a person farts during prayers? According to an ancient manuscript from Israel: If a man is standing saying a prayer, and he breaks wind, he must wait until the odor passes and begin praying all over again.

Over in India, though, farts are a method to attain enlightenment, through a yogi practice called Goze. You clear your mind and body of evil by belching and farting over and over again, while chanting: "Glory to those outbursts which escape above and below."

Glory to farts! Amen.

FART DICTIONARY

Fart in Other Languages

European Languages

Albanian	pordhë	
Basque	puzker	
Belarusian	пердеть	*(perdet)*
Bosnian	prdnuti	
Bulgarian	пръдня	*(prdnya)*
Catalan	pet	
Croatian	prdnuti	
Czech	prd	
Danish	prut	
Dutch	scheet	
Estonian	Pieru	
Finnish	pieru	
French	pet	
Galician	peidos	
German	Furz	
Greek	κλανιά	*(klaniá)*
Hungarian	fing	
Icelandic	prumpa	
Irish	broim	
Italian	scoreggia	
Latvian	pirst	
Lithuanian	bezdalius	
Macedonian	прдеж	*(prdej)*
Maltese	fiswa	

123

Norwegian	promp	
Polish	pierdnięcie	
Portuguese	peidar	
Romanian	bășina	
Russian	пердеть	*(perdet)*
Serbian	прднути	*(prdnuti)*
Slovak	prd	
Slovenian	prdec	
Spanish	pedo	
Swedish	fisa	
Ukrainian	пердіти	*(perdity)*
Welsh	rhech	
Yiddish	פֿאַרצן	*(fartsn)*

Middle Eastern Languages

Arabic	إلى ضرطة	*(durta)*
Armenian	**առել**	*(trrel)*
Azerbaijani	osurmaq	
Georgian	გავუშვა	*(gak'ueba)*
Hebrew	לְהַפְלִיץ	*(lehaplis)*
Persian	گوز	*(guwz)*
Turkish	osuruk	

Asian Languages

Bengali	বাতকর্ম	*(bātakarma)*
Burmese	လေလည်	*(lay lai)*
Cantonese	放屁	*(fong pei)*
Gujarati	અશિષ્ટ પ્રયોગ	*(asisista prayōga)*
Hindi	अपान वायु	*(apaan vaayu)*
Hmong	tso paus	
Japanese	おなら	*(onara)*
Kannada	ಹೂಸುಬಿಡು	*(hūsubidu)*
Kazakh	осыру	*(ociru)*
Khmer	ផោម	*(phaom)*
Korean	방귀	*(bang gwi)*
Lao	ຕົດ	*(tod)*
Malayalam	വളി	*(vali)*
Mandarin	屁	*(pì)*
Marathi	वाळीत टाकणे	*(vālīta tākanē)*
Mongolian	унгас	*(ungas)*
Nepali	फर्ट	*(pharta)*
Tajik	Форт	*(fort)*
Tamil	குசு	*(kusu)*
Telugu	అపానవాయువు	*(apānavāyuvu)*
Thai	ผายลม	*(phāylm)*
Urdu	پادری	*(paadna)*
Uzbek	osuruk	
Vietnamese	đánh rắm	

African Languages

Afrikaans	poep
Chichewa	amatulutsa fungo
Hausa	yí túusàa
Igbo	oku
Kinyarwanda	gusura
Sesotho	khilna
Somali	dhuusada
Swahili	jamba
Xhosa	nomfutho
Yoruba	ipa
Zulu	umfutho

Austronesian Languages

Cebuano	utot
Filipino	umut-ot
Hawaiian	pūhi'u
Indonesian	kentut
Javanese	ngentut
Kiribati	ting
Malagasy	vahana
Malay	kentut
Maori	pīhau
Samoan	saosaoa

American Languages

Cheyenne	pánestse
Haitian Creole	fè yon pete
Navajo	hadilzééh
Ojibwe	boogidi

Other Languages

Esperanto	furzo
Latin	crepitu

References

Kids Jailed for Farting
reason.com/blog/2012/11/29/the-town-where-farting-can-land-a-kid-in

Fart Tax Protest
www.theguardian.com/world/2003/sep/05/australia.davidfickling

Barn Burner
metro.co.uk/2014/01/28/barn-explodes-due-to-farting-cows-4280780

Crazy Toot Trial
www.citylab.com/equity/2017/10/berlin-fart-crazy-toot-trial-police/542766

Swedish Squealers
www.telegraph.co.uk/news/worldnews/europe/sweden/7520961/Swedish-prisoner-warned-over-flatulence-protests.html

www.theguardian.com/world/2016/mar/31/swedish-police-dismiss-case-of-the-revenge-fart

The Fart Before Christmas
fox42kptm.com/archive/santa-accused-of-spreading-his-holiday-flatulence-downtown

Fossil Farts
www.sciencenews.org/article/lemonade-broken-amber

Fart Bird
www.etymonline.com/word/partridge

Dog Fart Science
blogs.scientificamerican.com/dog-spies/things-to-know-on-dog-farting-awareness-day

Pennsylvania Cat Farts
  www.pawculture.com/pet-wellness/nutrition/do-cats-fart
  mousebreath.com/pennsylvanians-want-to-know-do-cats-fart

Pig Fart Emergency
  www.telegraph.co.uk/news/newstopics/howaboutthat/
  6669425/Flatulent-pig-sparks-gas-leak-scare.html

Turtle Fart Alarm
  metro.co.uk/2006/12/27/brussels-sprouts-cause-turtle-
  fart-alarm-3433537

Green Kangaroo Farts
  www.sciencenewsforstudents.org/article/kangaroos-have-
  green-farts
  www.theguardian.com/science/2015/nov/05/kangaroo-
  farts-could-have-implications-for-farmers-in-climate-
  change-fight

Death by Moth Fart
  wired.com/2015/06/silent-deadly-fatal-farts-immobilize-prey

Mermaid Farts
  www.livescience.com/43938-coral-snakes-colors-bites-
  farts-facts.html

National Chicken Farts
  foreignpolicy.com/2014/01/31/chinas-chicken-fart-decade

Farting Plants
  www.newscientist.com/article/mg22930554-800-farting-
  plants-have-a-built-in-stink-bomb-that-deters-predators
  en.wikipedia.org/wiki/Jacobaea_vulgaris
  en.wikipedia.org/wiki/Onopordum_acanthium

Shower Stink
  www.youtube.com/watch?v=B3zqFJDJf2Q

Fart Sniffing Robots
  news.xinhuanet.com/english/2016-04/10/c_135265651.htm
  dl.acm.org/citation.cfm?id=1961019

Sweet Farts
www.pilulepet.com/en

Fart Collecting
www.heptune.com/farts.html

Nurse Farts
www.ncbi.nlm.nih.gov/pmc/articles/PMC1121900

Fart Jars
mentalfloss.com/article/93132/fart-jars-17th-century-europe

Toot Tracker
www.popsci.com/smart-pill-gassy

Sir Henry the Farter
www.earlystuartlibels.net/htdocs/parliament_fart_section/C1i.html

The Forgotten Fart
Aubrey, John. Aubrey's Brief Lives
en.wikiquote.org/wiki/Edward_de_Vere

Abe Lincoln's Fart Jokes
www.washingtonpost.com/blogs/compost/post/8-of-abraham-lincolns-worst-joke-stories

Fart at the French
www.dailyedge.ie/colin-furze-fart-at-france-mechanical-arse-1586861-Jul2014

www.youtube.com/watch?v=7Ydv9Ef-99I

Queen of Farts
www.dailymail.co.uk/news/article-4546434/Queen-Victoria-ate-six-course-dinners.html

Mozart: A Little Fart Music
mentalfloss.com/article/55247/3-dirty-songs-mozart
lettersofnote.com/2012/07/oh-my-ass-burns-like-fire.html
mozart.com/en/blog/all/events/mozart-quotations-part-2

Royal Farter
en.wikipedia.org/wiki/Roland_the_Farter

French Fartiste
www.damninteresting.com/professional-farters

*www.slate.com/articles/health_and_science/medical_
examiner/2017/07/farting_lessons_from_flatulence_
artists_joseph_pujol.html*

Irish Rectal Music
*Ramsey, Greer. A Breath of Fresh Air: Rectal Music in Gaelic
Ireland. Archaeology Ireland, Vol. 16, No. 1, pp. 22-23*

*irishecho.com/2011/02/hows-the-craic-you-dont-want-to-
know-2*

Fart Songs
earlymusicmuse.com/a-brief-history-of-farting

Fart Symphony
*www.nydailynews.com/news/world/man-turns-fart-
recording-symphony-rectum-opus-article-1.2227538*

Farts on the Silver Screen
www.imdb.com/event/ev0000386/2003/1

Greek Reek
*en.antiquitatem.com/thunder-fart-aristophanes-clouds-
socrate*

*www.perseus.tufts.edu/hopper/
text?doc=Perseus:text:1999.01.0032:card=209*

*www.perseus.tufts.edu/hopper/
text?doc=Perseus:text:1999.01.0040:card=651*

Arabian Night Farts
*ia801002.us.archive.org/11/items/Abuhassan_201309/
abuhassan.mp3*

Divine Flatulence
www.shmoop.com/inferno/canto-xxi-summary.html

Rumbling Rabelais
www.menshealth.com/guy-wisdom/history-of-farts

Lilli-poot
www.booktryst.com/2012/05/jonathan-swift-on-women-who-fart-or.html

Franklin Farts Proudly
en.wikipedia.org/wiki/Fart_Proudly

teachingamericanhistory.org/library/document/to-the-royal-academy-of-farting

Hemingway's Heart Fart
Hemingway, Ernest. 88 Poems.

A Fart Parable
www.researchgate.net/publication/313903047

The Zen of Farting
www.avani-mehta.com/2008/08/08/how-fart-can-make-you-grow-spiritually-su-dongpos-story

Farts vs. Devils
churchpop.com/2014/08/10/29-of-martin-luthers-most-hiliariously-over-the-top-insults

Northern Farts
listverse.com/2017/02/09/10-weirdly-specific-gods-your-mythology-class-left-out

en.wikipedia.org/wiki/Matshishkapeu

Glory to Farts
The Alphabet of Ben Sira

Classen, Constance, David Howe, and Anthony Synott. Aroma: the Cultural History of Smell.

Edwardes, Allen. The Jewel in the Lotus.

popanth.com/article/silent-but-deadly-farts-across-cultures

Who writes this stuff?

M.D. WHALEN (writer)

He was always the kid who sat in the back of the class scribbling stories and cartoons. Later he sat in front of the class scribbling stories, when he should have been teaching! Now he writes full time in the back of his house, and has published many books under other names. He also enjoys cycling, world travel, and making rude noises in different languages.

FLORENTINO GOPEZ (artist)

His career began at age 6, when his cousin discovered him drawing on the ground with barbecue sticks. He wisely switched to pencils and pens, and has since worked all over the world and won awards as an animator and illustrator. His guitar and ukulele playing are as funny as his drawing.

Blast your Fart IQ with Farty Facts volume one!

Fish fart. Astronauts fart more. Even dead people fart. Ancient fart jokes, farts that started wars, farts around the world.

All this and more in the original poot-powered Big Book of Farty Facts!

Know the facts?
Now read the stories!

Can Willy and Peter defeat the evil clowns and save all humanity from ex-*stink*-tion with Weapons of Mass Flatulation?

Willy and Peter blast their way into space. But do they have enough gas in their guts to repel an invasion of farting aliens from Uranus?

JOIN US!

FARTY FARTERS CLUB*

WWW.FARTBOYS.COM

*Even girls are allowed!